THE
NOT-SO-SPOOKY
SILENT
LETTERS

PHONICS READ-ALOUDS

Title: The Not-So-Spooky Silent Letters
ISBN: 9798325192937
First Published in the United States of America, 2024

Contributors: Manns, Yvette, author; Blu, Ana K. illustrator

Summary: The ghost letters GN, KN, MB and WR meet the vowels and teach them about silent letter pairs. They work together to build new words along with the consonants and expand word building possibilities.

www.PhonicsReadAlouds.com

THE NOT-SO-SPOOKY
SILENT LETTERS

Written by: Yvette Manns
Illustrated by: Ana K. Blu

It was a dark and stormy night in Vowel Valley. The vowels were tucked under their knit blankets after a long day of building words with their consonant friends.

Right before U drifted off to sleep, a glow in the distance caught his eye. Two miles away stood a spooky, old castle. There was a bright light coming from the window and U just had to know what it was!

U got dressed, combed his hair and went to check on the other vowels. He knocked on A, E, I, and O's bedroom doors.

 A was kneading dough to bake bread.

 E was knitting a scarf for her aunt.

 I was writing a letter to his pen pal.

 O was practicing his wrestling moves.

U said, "Since we're all awake from the storm, let's find out what's going on at that spooky castle." A agreed, "I'm always up for an adventure!"

When they arrived at the doorstep of the castle, they noticed a wrinkled paper on the doorstep that read, "Please Knock and Enter." A moved a wreath out of the way to knock on the door, but no one answered. She knocked harder, but her knuckles began to hurt so she stopped.

I interrupted, "I know what we should do. Let's turn the knob and see if the door is unlocked."

I twisted the doorknob until his wrist got sore, but the door wouldn't open.

U knelt down and said, "Maybe we can check for a spare key." He found an old key hidden under a garden gnome. I inserted the key in the lock and the large wooden door creaked open.

The vowels tiptoed into the castle. E exclaimed, "Is anyone home?"

They were starting to think that entering this castle was a bad idea.

They wrung their hands nervously and began to sweat. They felt like their stomachs were in knots!

All of a sudden, they heard a voice whisper, "We've been waiting for you."

The vowels got so spooked that they ran for the door to escape! They crashed into a large statue of a knight wrapped in metal. When they looked behind them, they saw someone in the shadows. "Aaahhh!," A screamed. "A ghost!"

The ghost replied, "What's wrong? No need to worry, I'm a friendly ghost. I wanted to meet some new friends so I turned my bright sign towards Vowel Valley for you to see!" The ghost unwrapped its cape and showed them the letters "KN" on its sheet. I exclaimed, "Wow, you have letters just like us!"

"Yes, I have a pair of letters written on me, KN, but you only hear one sound - the /n/ sound!" KN explained. "Meet the other ghosts - GN, WR and MB. They're silent letter pairs, too."

O asked, "What are silent letter pairs?"

WR explained, "Silent letter pairs are special consonants. When we are next to each other in the same syllable, one letter is silent. For example, the W in WR is silent, like in the words 'wrong', 'wrap' and 'wreck'."

"Since you're ghosts and pairs of consonants that have one silent sound, where is GH?" O asked.

GN answered, "Great question! GH actually has three different jobs."

"Sometimes GH represents /f/ like the last sound we hear in laugh."

"Also, in words like night and taught, GH is completely silent."

"At other times, you only hear GH's /g/ sound in words like in ghost and ghoul, but only at the beginning of words. That's when our friend GH likes to come visit us!"

U suggested, "Well, if ghost letters are made of consonants, would you like to meet our other consonant friends? We can invite them to meet us near Vowel Valley and we can build some words together!" MB ghost gave U the thumbs-up sign.

The vowels, silent ghost letters and consonants met at the top of the hill. They all worked together to build the words wren, lamb, knee and sign. They had so much fun building words all night long!

"Well, ghosts," U said, "it turns out that you weren't so spooky after all. You just needed to teach us about silent letters. Now, readers have new words they can spell because of you! How does that make you feel?"

TIPS FOR AFTER READING

- **Go on a word hunt and list all the words in this story with silent letter pairs.**
- **Sort the words you find by KN, GN, WR or MB and share with a classmate.**
- **Read all the words with silent letter pairs out loud.**
- **Using another passage or text, highlight all the words with silent letter pairs that you can find.**
- **Look for words that have a silent letter, but do not have silent letter pairs.**

FUN FACTS ABOUT
SILENT LETTER PAIRS

- Silent letter pairs are two consonants next to each other in one syllable that represent one of their sounds.
- KN, GN, MB and WR are some of the most common silent letter pairs.
- There are other letters that can be silent letter pairs, such as BT and RH. When B is before T, the B is silent, as in "doubt". When R is before H, the H is silent, as in "rhombus".
- Words with WR can be related to bending, turning or twisting, such as wring or wrestle.
- Words with KN can be related to something sharp or pointy, such as knee or knife.
- Sometimes single letters can be silent too, such as the E in cake, the H in honest, the N in autumn, the S in island, the T in listen, the P in pterodactyl, the W in two and much more!
- Here are some more words that have silent letter pairs:

> climb crumb design gnat gnaw gnome knee knit
> know knuckles lamb sign thumb wrap wreck wrote

CAN YOU THINK OF ANY MORE WORDS
WITH SILENT LETTER PAIRS?

CHECK OUT OTHER BOOKS IN THE SERIES!

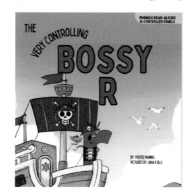

...and more books!

STAY IN THE KNOW!

Visit
www.PhonicsReadAlouds.com
for activities, stickers and more!

DID YOU ENJOY THIS STORY?

★★★★★

Please consider leaving us a review on Amazon. This helps us to learn what you want to read about next and tell other people about our stories!

Made in the USA
Las Vegas, NV
25 November 2024